Nasty Water

Collected New Orleans Poems

Nasty Water

Collected New Orleans Poems

James Nolan

2018
University of Louisiana at Lafayette Press

Also by James Nolan

Poetry

Why I Live in the Forest (Wesleyan University Press)
What Moves Is Not the Wind (Wesleyan University Press)
Drunk on Salt (Willow Springs Editions)

Fiction

You Don't Know Me: New and Selected Stories
(University of Louisiana at Lafayette Press)
Higher Ground (University of Louisiana at Lafayette Press)
Perpetual Care: Stories (Jefferson Press)

Memoir

Flight Risk: Memoirs of a New Orleans Bad Boy
(University Press of Mississippi)

Poetry in Translation

Pablo Neruda, Stones of the Sky (Copper Canyon Press)
Jaime Gil de Biedma, Longing: Selected Poems
(City Lights Books)

Criticism

*Poet-Chief: The Native American Poetics of Walt Whitman
and Pablo Neruda* (University of New Mexico Press)

Essays

*Fumadores en manos de un dios enfurecido: Ensayos
al caballo entre varios mundos* (Madrid: Editores Enigma)

for jazz percussionist and writer Charles Suhor,
my teacher at Benjamin Franklin High School
who first inspired me to write poetry

© 2018 by University of Louisiana at Lafayette Press
All rights reserved

ISBN 13 (paper): 978-1-935754-64-0

http://ulpress.org
University of Louisiana at Lafayette Press
P.O. Box 40831
Lafayette, LA 70504-0831

Printed on acid-free paper in the United States.

Cover photo: Sandra Russell Clark.
Author photo: Doug Parker.

Library of Congress Cataloging-in-Publication Data

Names: Nolan, James, 1947- author.
Title: Nasty water : collected New Orleans poems, (1968-2016) / James Nolan.
Description: Lafayette, LA : University of Louisiana at Lafayette Press, 2018.
Identifiers: LCCN 2018023729 | ISBN 9781946160355
Subjects: LCSH: New Orleans (La.)--Poetry.
Classification: LCC PS3564.O36 A6 2018 | DDC 811/.54--dc23
LC record available at https://lccn.loc.gov/2018023729

Contents

Preface ix

I: Lost Child

Shotgun Nocturne for Those Who Left 3
Return to the House of Scorpio 4
Mardi Gras Grandmothers 6
The Invention of Hands on Columbus Street 9
Mirror Tango 10
Japanese Plums 12
In the Rotunda 14
Judgment 15
The Silent Piano 16
Figure at the Fireplace 17
Dream Castle (1964) 18
Hunt & Peck 19
The Cage 20
The Shoebox 23
How to Keep It 24
Presenting Eustacia Beauchaud: Rosary 3 25
Tyger! Tyger! 27
Locked in a Home for *les Enfants Dérangés par Dieu* 29
Time Explains, Among Other Things 30
The American Century 31
Sum 34
Dead Man's Float 36
Home Blues 37
Cold Front 39

Reading Poetry at the Maple Leaf Bar
   from a Book I Haven't Written Yet 40

II: When The Saints

Over the Oysters 43
Nasty Water 44
Crabs in a Hamper 47
Acts of God 48
Superdome Lullaby 49
A Blind Lady Singing 50
From Below, from Above 51
King Midas Blues 52
Pelicans Feeding 53
Spell for This First Kiss 54
French Quarter Bar Fugue 55
My Wild Lover 59
Iron Lace 61
Nietzsche in Disneyland 62
Hitting the Carnival Wall 63
The Princess of Banana Leaves and Rain 64
Lament on the Assassination Six Days Later 66
Mr. Boudreaux's Civil War 68
Solomon's Sword, or the Café au Lait Blues 71
What Remains 72
Impossible Cases 73
Busted Flat in Baton Rouge 75
In Lieu of Flowers 76
Visit to the Memory Unit 78
Waveland 79

Acknowledgements 81
About the Author 83

Preface
Autobiography of Place

De la musique avant toute chose...
-Paul Verlaine, "Art poétique"

After moving home to New Orleans in 1996, I became a regular in the city's then burgeoning poetry reading scene, often performing my poems with musical accompaniment at venues such as Café Brasil, the Dragon's Den, Funky Butt, Gold Mine, Maple Leaf, Palm Court, and other clubs. For a long time, these joints were jumping. The poem that always received the most rapturous response, before and especially after Hurricane Katrina, was a New Orleans anthem called "Nasty Water." For a while it seemed as if I'd forever be known, like Al "Carnival Time" Johnson and Ernie "Mother-in-Law" K Doe, as James "Nasty Water" Nolan.

So I had no trouble choosing a title for this half-century collection of fifty New Orleans-themed poems, a book I consider an autobiography of place. Of course, it was no coincidence that I ventured to perform my poems with guitarists, singers, pianists, flutists, and percussionists, because these words are steeped in a native musicality that I must have absorbed as a boy from the mirliton vines I picked or the soggy crab grass I weeded. Almost every time I read one of these poems aloud I hear an instrument playing in the background: a saxophone wailing on a street corner, a guitar echoing inside a courtyard, or piano chords drifting from behind a half-closed shutter.

The first half of the book is chronologically autobiographical, and can be read as a poetic companion to my recent book *Flight Risk: Memoirs of a New Orleans Bad Boy*. Some of these poems were written in the heat of the times—certainly those four dated to my incarceration in St. Vincent DePaul Hospital in 1968—

but most are a wistful look back at childhood and adolescence inspired by translating Pablo Neruda's poetic memoir, *Memorial de Isla Negra*. The second section of poems is an orchestration of New Orleans culture in general as I've experienced it during the past decades. Several of these poems are dated in historical moments: Martin Luther King's assassination, Hurricane Katrina, the Gulf oil spill, and the terrorist attack on 9/11, which, as fate would have it, occurred during a Formosan termite restoration upending my life in the French Quarter. And now, of course, the present era of mass tourism. It's not always clear in these poems where the "I" ends and the history and culture of place take over.

That's when you know a whole tribe is speaking.

When you ask New Orleanians a question, we won't give you a direct opinion but either will tell you a story or sing you a song. I've published my New Orleans stories elsewhere, but here are my songs. I hope you're attuned to the music and moved to read the poems aloud, as they were meant to be experienced. Over the years my fraught relationship with this city, its past, my deeply rooted family, and my own place here has been both a torturous and a celebratory one. These poems represent a complex coming to terms with where "I—/ for lack of a better word / a better world—/ belong."

New Orleans, 2018

I.

Lost Child

*At moments I think
of the child who lived in me
and ask him a favor,
maybe that he just look at me
to acknowledge I was once him
and now speak with his tongue*

*but from the charred wreck of hours
he stares straight at my face
and does not recognize me.*

- Pablo Neruda, "Lost Child"

Shotgun Nocturne for Those Who Left

for Aimée Bagur in Santa Cruz

Hands folded, you sit in communion white,
your presence a stilled courtyard
as I pace the deck, talking of home.
Our memories merge, lend substance:
we're related by the mirliton vine.
Pale Californian pastels peel back
like buckled sheetrock after a flood.

Inside the walls of an abandoned house
a Gulf breeze billowing filmy curtains.
Footsteps on the gallery. A screen door slams.
The furniture covered, stiff with restraint.
We're rummaging for something they forgot
to give us, examining dust for prayers.

At sundown the old woman next door shouts
in Cajun French to her family, all dead,
winning the same old arguments again.
Two children remain on the swing set
weaving shadows of live oak into evening.
When we left, they stayed—and the hands
of the hall clock stuck as it struck that hour.

Any minute Mémère will be back for them,
slice a lemon in two and dip it in sugar.
Streetlamps go on but they're obedient
as the last sentinels of a lost country.
And even though we stumble for decades
through seasonless landscapes, they wait.

The porch light beckons, alive with moths.

Return to the House of Scorpio

Walking again down Canal Street
in this seething Scorpio city:
you never really leave New Orleans,
you only dream you do.

With surprise attacks
of comfort I sit back—
can maneuver drunk
the inkwell spiral stairs

a struck match throwing Fellini
shadows against the peeling walls.
Under high superstitious ceilings
I reach right for the café au lait

there where hot red peppers dry
strung along the kitchen mantel.
I even know the black cat by name:
come here, Minou . . . Minou.

The smell of garlic and onions,
of oysters and simmering red beans!
And where have I heard that
tough Brooklyn talk before?

New Orleans, I can see you
faded ageing whore you are,
Blanche DuBois in a pinafore
primping in the armoire mirror:

crow's-feet in amber lantern light.
Mother, through every half-shut
shutter I see your marquisette face
in damp courtyards of hydrangea

and Father, it's your voice I hear
call down around Magazine Street
when my cheeks are flushing red
in some boozy Irish brawl.

MARDI GRAS GRANDMOTHERS:
Portrait in Red and Black Crayon

As I see them now and then:
one was fat and one was thin,
one pushed me out, one held me in.

One created family disgraces,
dyed her hair red and danced
her way to Acapulco making
clown lipstick faces.
The other wore mourning
and old Creole laces

the two grandmothers I had.

*

My Irish grandmother,
big Nana of the rose hats
and spaghetti-strap dresses,
danced on Mardi Gras floats
until she was seventy-five
with her bonbon hairdos
and her high-gloss Plymouth
and her hot hotel suite.
With her great dripping chins,
she was a languishing sea turtle
in the parade of Iris.

Ji-my Ji-my
she would siren to me
over the flambeau carriers
from her tinsel perch
as lush Queen of the Nile.
And I would be hoisted up,
smacked with a bourbon kiss,
and showered with a gob
of gorgeous glass light.

*

My French grandmother gripped me tight,
wrapped her old salvation coat
around her parchment face
and held me back from slipping
into the streams of flambeau carriers
oh I could march with them all night.
Hip-swaying flame bandits
prancing in a Dixie highstep
rhythm that made my feet
start tapping on the curb.

Mémère wanted it to be Ash Wednesday,
to get back to her washing load.
She liked to see the first communions
filing into church in starched white frills.
She liked to think the Virgin Mother
had held pins in her mouth while hemming them.

But I would always buck loose
to follow Nana's gargoyle smile
and jig with packs of black kids
clamoring for kewpies in midair

until I shouldered back and sank
into the surf of shouting as
flambeaux streaked off around the block
and broken beads crackled everywhere.

*

And I knew that she'd be standing there
shadowed under street lamps in her coat
waiting in the rubbled paper trash,

collar buttoned high around her throat

knew that she would take the outstretched hand
hot from grabbing glass beads from the floats,
take the dazzled face, the jazzed-out legs,
take the eyes that panicked through the crowd

and with the votive candle of her heart
lead her flambeau boy the dark way home.

The Invention of Hands on Columbus Street

Then our household gods were handless saints
whose imported porcelain faces bore down
from the mahogany mantle and prie-dieu
as the Sunday radio rosary droned on
to beads fingered in a circle, rocking.

Blue Limoges arms of the Queen of Heaven,
scarlet arms of the Sacred Heart of Jesus,
ended in sockets where hands should be—
gaping holes into which, I swear, spiders
and roaches scampered when lights snapped on.

Breaking so easily, the hands were shipped
separately and never arrived from France
or were stolen by voodoos looking for powers:
voodoo altars piled high with plaster hands,
handless saints filled with cockroach wings.

Pale boy in a polo shirt, I circled those rooms,
acquainted as an alley lizard with damp silence.
I liked to hide behind clapboard corner churches
to hear gospel fill the sky with fluttering robes.
Clapping, I joined the saints come marching in

and earned these two hands popping fingers to glory.
The child's story ends here, with the invention of hands.
Sometimes I go back, powerless as a Sunday afternoon
when shuttered sunlight casts its spell of powders
and I dream of saints' hands, boxes full of holiness,

lost for generations, marked *fragile, expédite.*

Mirror Tango

He'd studied, I
studied Latin
from his books. He'd
collected, I collected
stamps in his album.
I painted what he'd
painted, swam at the Y
where he had swum.
He was the other Jimmy,
run over by a funeral
parlor hearse (I'm not
making this up). He
departed at sixteen—
so did I, but have yet
to reach the other
country, though I try.

He was café au lait
as a Creole, I fair
as a Celt. He was good—
Boy Scout, paper route—I bad
as a marijuana seed. When I
raised my right, he his left,
when I turned east, he west
in our dyslexic tango.
We slept together in
his twin bed, my dead uncle
and I, my mother's brother
and I. When they called
"Jimmy" they meant me
but he followed. The toys
were his. He let me play.

At times I hoist a tent
of fire around myself,

laugh, gulp light, love
women, but the flames
go out. There he is, waiting
in the shadows of another
man's face watching mine.
"Come back," I summon,
tangoing alone with him,
my body his but another's,
his body mine but not there.
Then I curl up to sleep
with my dark double
who named me during
a hurricane long ago.

Japanese Plums

When they chopped them down
something unraveled
like the catcher's mitt
of a ten-year-old's heart.
Didn't they see the stone circles
I'd built around the trees?
Then I kept so many secrets
with the earth, names of plants
and African countries, clay castles
in crawfish chimneys, continents
in live oak roots.

          By the time
I got home from school
they'd chain-sawed them all,
cemented the yard, "better
for kids," they said.
We fought with the landlord
and the next month packed.
This was when I first
realized the world outside
exists more than I do: a war.
I've camouflaged myself
among lost Japanese plums
as I sign treaties
with concrete.

          And suddenly
in Spain, on the terrace
of this house I happen
to be living in, a Japanese
plum tree in a tin washtub
leaps out like a burning bush,
yellow, gnarled. I reach
to pluck the sweet, spitting

slippery pits in arches
into the street:

                    victory
of Biblical patience
and an impossible love.

In The Rotunda

How awful to be shot
by a doctor in the rotunda,
I thought climbing the steps
to our glorious capitol at eleven,
not listening, as usual,
to anything the teacher said
about Huey P. Long, wondering
where oh where is my rotunda—
or do I even have a rotunda?—
like other body parts sticking out
nobody ever told me about.
Maybe only big fat governors
with cigars had rotundas: shots,
doctors, it all gave me the creeps.

The best part was the gift shop
where I bought a souvenir cigar
then lit it up high on top
of the capitol building, smoking
like a real politician, dreaming
of Huck Finn on the Mississippi,
other territories beyond the bridge:
New Orleans boy on his first field
trip with no idea how far afield life
would lead him, puking up his grits
all over Baton Rouge, Louisiana,

sick to his rotunda.

Judgement

Fifty years ago, while standing in his bathrobe,
grand-oncle Auguste was disowned from *la famille Créole*
after announcing his marriage to a Goddamn Yankee Protestant.
My grandmother, in the middle of pressing his linen suit,
threw it in the corner to give to the vegetable man,
crossed herself harshly then went on to chop parsley.
No one spoke to him or of him for half a century.
The silence was golden: he lived down the block.

Last year Uncle Auguste raced down our hall in his bathrobe
shouting, "Where's the white linen suit you were ironing?"
My grandmother dropped dead in the bathtub, that being that.
Uncle Auguste never did renounce the Protestant Reformation,
never did renounce the Union Army or his Vermont wife.
He was never one for details. They say he didn't care.
By now his bathrobe is frayed and flecked with lintballs
as he stands on his front gallery muttering to himself

like a man let out of a taxi at the wrong corner
in the wrong city of the wrong century,
waiting for a change of clothes
and wondering what went wrong.

The Silent Piano

Grande-grande-Mémère was playing Chopin
on the night Lincoln was shot. A Union soldier,
Reconstructing, advised her please to stop.
"Merci pour la visite mais je ne comprends pas."
And she proceeded with her Chopin
on the night Lincoln was shot.

The second time the Yankee came by
she showed him to the door. Drunk
or rude, he would not spoil her tropical
étude. Then back he came with a hammer
and a sack of rusty spikes to nail the piano
shut, tight as a coffin top. Not a note

of music has been played on it
since the night Lincoln was shot.

Figure at the Fireplace

In high button boots and striped suspenders
they rocked side by side at the hallway chimney
and I sidestepped them, uncles whose names
I seldom spoke—Manuel, Henri—or faces saw,
far from the family hoopla, on the other

side of doors: at the end of a murky corridor
a solemn corner of bachelor smoke and ashes,
survivors in a world they'd given up on,
shadows across the lemon layer cake
of Sunday afternoons on Bayou Road.

When they did talk, it was of some war.
I was never really sure if they worked
or where, yet how ominously they sailed
through weekdays in the same black vests
with as little to do with 1952 as possible.

And just this afternoon, that expression
on a boy's face as he watched me at the grate,
as if he had found a root twisted inside
the cherry-wood table, a bullet in the roast,
a shroud among the jackets on the coat rack.

Those uncles never told me their stories
and how could I tell this child mine?
Perhaps a look suffices—a cold appraisal
of the charcoal in the flesh—by eyes
that have stared too long into the fire.

Dream Castle (1964)

for Harriete Grissom

That jive night years ago,
remember? when we stumbled
blind-drunk from a dive
on Frenchmen Street

I with boy's first beard,
you in first high heels.
The Dream Castle: illegal
integrated Marigny

bar where we gulped
underage booze, vibrating
to Babe Stovall's steel
guitar, school books

stashed, afraid of a raid,
we stayed on even after
the old white bohos split.
We were in Tangiers,

a cheap Paris café.
We blinked our eyes,
we turned the page.
Reeling with sky

we rolled with Rimbaud
down the neutral ground
on Esplanade: sixteen,
smart as shit, dumb

with sudden wonder.

Hunt & Peck

> *And at that age poetry came around*
> *to look for me...*
> -Pablo Neruda, "Poetry"

A permanent detour, these pages.

I wanted to play the blues or paint
but we had no piano, no canvasses,
even less any money for lessons or oils.
Then I discovered it cobwebbed in
the basement: Pepère's Royal typewriter
from his tobacco shop on Chartres Street,
drawing my fingers to its clacky wail.

I played those fat round black keys
like Ray Charles belting out Van Gogh,
peering through glass side panels
to understand where words come from,
shuttling back and forth on a loom,
pecking at myself, searching the page
for an uncracked voice, another face.

What I pulled out of that cantankerous
old contraption wasn't a song or sun-
flower but a map I'm still following,
mute landscapes in black-and-white.
And that skinny kid, jumping
awake from sheets of lost chords
and colors to write

has made the best of it.

THE CAGE

Like the medieval Bible
chained shut in the sacristy,
in those days sex was under
lock and key. Turning sixteen,
body at all-out civil war,
I would sneak up to The Cage
on the ninth tier of the Tulane library
where I worked after high school

to unlock the Page fence
and under a dangling bulb
sit cross-legged on the floor
devouring the *Kama Sutra*,
Havelock Ellis, *The Kinsey Report*,
even Terry Southern, scanning
indexes for words like *foreplay,
fellatio, cunnilingus, orgasm*

then descend the spiral steps
to attend to pinch-lipped students
as I drifted through arabesques
of harems, humping my way
through the Dewey Decimal System
with a creaky shelving cart
in the attic must of the stacks,
and swaying home on a streetcar

I'd study the white stocking
legs of the McKenzie Bakery lady
or the conductor's mustache reflected
in a slanted side window behind
his curtain, wondering if they knew
about the Elephant Position, "techniques
for mutual ecstasy," or the outer-labia.
I was weak-kneed in a greenhouse

of organs opening, pulsing, and closing
like the waxy genitals of tropical plants
while bodies around me were displayed
taboo as mangoes behind plate glass.
Night after night I would crouch in
The Cage, memorizing the floor plan
of the prison, deciphering the ruby
secret, this tattoo in my blood.

The Shoebox

What was it you kept in that shoebox,
the white shoebox on the closet top shelf?
What is it that has kept you so long,
Father? in the box filled with photographs
of the concentration camps you liberated,
the box that trembles like Pandora's
with a thousand black moths beating
against a blackened screen: the mute
tremulous scream, 16-millimeter
with the sound shut off.

When my sister and I slipped into your room
to take it from the shelf and deal
the photographs out like playing cards
on the floor

this trench to me
that heap to her

that bit of hair
this bit of bone

when we dealt it out like the fortunes,
children squat-legged on the rug,
official details of official skeletons

we always came across
the dog-eared one of you
hunched in a belted coat,
squinting and standing aside
to help into a transport van
the wizened prisoner nearby
who had lived four years
like an animal in a crate

who beckons you from the shelf,
shuffled back into a shoebox

that I've seen you open
and close behind closed lids,
the jerky, grainy footage
that loops through your mind,
the shoebox in the closet
where you keep all your pain.

I remember the musty stink
of the old German armband
I tried to have cleaned
at the cleaners one day;
the feel of kerosene and ash
on that grimy red rag
of a huge Nazi flag
big as the living room rug;
the dark steel-foundry weight
of that black bludgeon Luger
dead as a brick in your drawer;
of the souvenir sword hung over my bed,
the contained vision of hideousness
hung all over the house.

I have seen you try to rest
like someone who has just cleaned the house;
like someone who has just cleaned the world,
who knows there is no rest, you sometimes rest
where I have put you, in a white shoebox
in which you sit forever now
staring into a white shoebox in your lap
fascinated to rearrange the cards
in a losing hand of solitaire
played over and over again

that you cannot win, I cannot win
but box within box within box
is put away,
              is never put away.

How To Keep It

My mother told me once of love.
She told me what it is
and how to keep it
(Isaiah she quoted, Isaiah taught her)

so when she signed the papers
to lock me in and up
she bit her glove a while
but knew what she was doing.
She pocketed the doctor's smile
and played with it like clay
sitting alone in her lavender room
beside the phone and my sixth-grade picture.

My window now is barred with iron,
the gate is stronger.
Her heart is like a pumpkin shell
and that should keep her.

(St. Vincent DePaul Hospital, January 1968)

Presenting Eustacia Beauchaud: Rosary 3

Eustacia Beauchaud
combed her bozo
red wig into the Frenchiest
of twists and never missed.
Shot down from Geriatrics
for alleged obscene advances
on a twice-stumped catatonic,
she cousined all the kookies
on the spot and said her name
meant good and hot.

In faded brocade she flung
her years, all seventy-six,
down the echoless hall
of Acutely Disturbed.
With a fox-trot flutter
and a Revlon wink
she gave us the word
that you're only as young
as you think, which lit
a few lima-bean eyes
dampened by months of therapy,
who caressed the gift
incomprehensively
then let it drop.

With rouge as thick as licorice
and some lipstick oulala
and that slightly oompah strut
(her spirits all played tubas)
she told us she was Lady Levee
and had spooned with Old Man River—
a plantation queen she had been
aunt of the mayor of New Orleans:

        "If I had my d'rathers,"
she sang,
        "I'd rather be down in old Louisiana."

The happy thump of her jazz piano
cured the bristly wino up the corridor
who gurgled her repertoire constantly
somewhere hot deep in his throat.

Evenings mounted like bordello
brawls down in Recreation Therapy.
"A Southern belle forgets like hell,"
I heard her hoot at the TV premiere
of *Hush . . . Hush Sweet Charlotte*
as she was being helped to the toilet.

Always around Individual Lockup
time she would tell the story ending
"pull his tail, the nigra told me,
that's how you get a horse to work,"
and then slap herself into a giddy-up with
        "We're just twenty-five minutes from Canal Street,
        let's go see the parade."
While orderlies jangled keys she finaled
by raising the beautiful varicose blue
of her leg to the keyboard to pick out "Dixie"
with the spiked heel of her pointed shoe

and then the black men in white
would put her to bed
for the night.

                (St. Vincent DePaul Hospital, January 1968)

Tyger! Tyger!

I hear the buckles rattle from the bed
wheeled in after midnight next to mine
and know the straps
could snap at any time
to hurl the madman
biting on my back.
I hear his nerve-clenched teeth
explode into the mattress
and see between the cowhide and the sheet
muscles strain like wire through paper flesh.
The floor around our beds
is spotted with the spittle of his hate:
the heavy padlock clangs in speech
so primitive that reptiles
crowd into his mouth
which makes no words
nor knows no way but burning.

Bound by the leather strap cut into his stomach,
bound by the hard metallic table, by a taste tied hard
in his mouth, he turns toward the wall groaning
within me, his face forming in my thin hands,
my boy's beard bristling
with his fever as we seem
drunk into the father breath
that breathed us both,
tiger and lamb, room-
mates in bedlam:
the ward is inside
out.

The room is dark,
sleek and tight

and crouches like an animal to strike,
he and I the gristled eyes
that cannot see each other
but move in the skull's willful sway
together.

(St. Vincent DePaul Hospital, January 1968)

Locked In A Home For
Les Enfants Dérangés Par Dieu

Madonna over the pool table,
moss-covered weathered cross
nailed to a sycamore tree
next to the volleyball court:

save yourself this moment
from the mad nuns twisted in nets
genuflecting to volley
and genuflecting to serve

from the lemon grey hands
of Mémère at her prie-dieu
dabbing drops of holy water
like perfume behind her ears

from those mumbling geriatrics
from whom trembling noviates remove
their rosaries and metal crucifixes
and other implements of suicide

from the spiked wind through the iron gate
from the house of your mothers and wives
and sisters and brothers all screaming
Your presence with lips worn thin by Your name

from the crowding El Greco faces
leaning green outside of my window
who beckon me through to their orchards
with a smile of their pale mute hands.

(St. Vincent DePaul Hospital, January 1968)

Time Explains, Among Other Things

that vast landscape
inverted into the gut
from the umbilicus. Parents.
Arch-demons with zigzag eyebrows.
Lavender goddesses tucked inside
martyred wings. Technicolored
pillars of ice and fire.

You are older. They come to visit.
You are peering down at two plump,
fussy pigeons awkward as adolescents
in your presence. For years, unnoticed,
they have sat behind you on the bus.
They need paper towels,
small jokes, special favors.

Whoever you thought
they were is who you became.
The drama has rubbed smooth
as a baby's butt, a bald head,
down to the human nub.
These geezers are good
for going to the movies with.

New loves play out their old stories,
arch eyes, explode in purple powders,
while parents, waiting on dinner, wonder
what the hell has gotten into you.

The American Century

in memory, Auguste Glaudot
(1864-1949)

You were just checking out
as I was checking in
   during those bouncy days
   when Europe was a heap
   of smoldering bricks.
And both of us were small, bald,
   wrinkled and almost toothless,
   dead set to have our ways
   with cushions and spoons:
an instant recognition
   between somebody nearly ninety
   and someone only one.
You made me *fait dodo*
   cooing in French to *le petit*
   crooked in the arm of your cardigan
as if you knew your 19th century dream
   of the *grande famille bourgeoise*
   would one day rest
   on my queer shoulder.

Those were the boom years:
   G.I. Joe with a bottle of booze
   and his boogie-woogie bungalow
   bride on the G.I. Bill.
In a snapshot of the shotgun
four generations of us shared
you hold me up like a prize trout,
   brand-new American doll,
   blond victory boy
awarded to a bow-tied immigrant
grown old, as poor and defeated
as your mother country had become.
   The world has changed, Pepère,
   in these past fifty years.

The Champs Elysées is glittering,
Canal Street a no man's land now.
   And your American doll,
    ton arrière-petit-fils,
has been a long time gone.

I've been leafing through the leathery
journal you kept during your 1889
   journey to Paris and Brussels,
    in fastidious Franglish, with such
     ambivalence about *les américains.*
But you came home, married a Creole,
swooped your bride up the steps
   of the Pontabala Apartments
   and sold cigars on Chartres.
Americans are good at starting over,
   they say—you wanted
    to stay away but couldn't

and neither could I.
   After eight years in Barcelona
   I'm back and don't know why,
rocking in my Spanish underwear,
living alone in the French Quarter
around the corner from where Mémère
was born, up to my elbows in okra,
   in charge of these shards
   of your *grande famille,*
   the tomb (just whitewashed)
   and mantle clock (still chiming)
of what's left of your furniture
   I strip and sand and oil
   until original energy
   shines through a veneer

blackened by war and Depression years.

I'm winding your Belle Époque
  clock where a bored bronze
  Mercury broods over the hour
as if nothing much has happened
in the past hundred years,
  as if all this time
  two ancient children
  had been playing checkers
  on the gallery
  lost in a reverie
  between our generations—
the first and the last—
waiting for the American
century to finally end.

(1999)

Sum

My accountant father
counts pebbles and lawn-
mowers and edges the grasses
with somber precision.
His life like machine tape
droops down in a white beard
and ends in a darkness
of double red figures
that mount like a staircase
toward some *ergo sum*.

With asterisk eyes braced
he dreams of a golf score.
Report cards and budgets
are good things to sleep on
except that they flutter
and need constant folding.
Calendrical suns stand
like forms left to fill in
as he considers the number
of hamburger patties still
stacked in the freezer.

My accountant father
made me count
one day to two
and I never made it through.

My accountant father
confides in his mother
that he really has nothing.
She calls up to ask us
about what he tells her:
we place all his things all
around where he'll be sure

to see them and count them
and sit waiting in three's.
We're all we can gather.

My accountant father
lies counting to sixty
and counting in two's
to fill up the nothing
of the second hand's shadow.

My daddy. Accounted.
A handful of pebbles.
He never was married,
divided or touched.

Dead Man's Float
in memory of my father

The wave lunging against the shore
along where the train is passing
freezes into a jagged salt tongue
while the passengers' mouths
stiffen wide open in midsentence
as I wander the aisle half-believing,
the last customer lost in a wax museum.

There, my daughter making up for the funeral,
my son going through my shirts and papers,
my wife, white knuckled, signing something,
a frieze of family, deaf mute, glazed ceramic,
drooping and swaying like wilted calla lilies
over the waxed-paper face under the veil.

I'm not there to see them shove the body
into the box onto the slab inside the tomb
to be held over the stinking Louisiana
ooze I fought with garden hose and broom.
Give it back to monkey grass and river sand.

Only I am going somewhere, flowing quickly,
quietly as water, but I don't know where,
as if the train were whooshing backwards
with the whirling sound a record makes
when the lights go out, winding down
to the woozy moan of a toneless cello.

Shapes drift by in time-lapsed bursts
caking over like mud baked in the sun
then cracking open to reveal what was
inside the masks I saw all along, and I—
how can I describe it?—I'm like . . .
it's like winning or sex or too much bourbon,

everything is still and I am everything.

Home Blues

You can hear trains
from the back porch
of my mother's house,
trains late at night
pulling into New Orleans
from the north,
from the south.

You can hear mourning
doves nested in
the waist-length hair
of dangling ferns,
those Creole ladies
who choke back grief
and coo a *hoohoohoo*
cool as river mist
as you slowly smoke
on the wooden porch
of my mother's house.

You can hear a cough
that guts the night
like a knife. Inside,
the lavender girl
from McDonogh High
who gave me birth
curled up like a leaf.
You can hear stalks
of dried hydrangea
rustle in the wind
from the winter porch
of my mother's house.

You can hear the dead regret,
the swamp sunk into itself,
the crawfish in its hole,
elephant ears listening
to a front door slammed
twenty-five years ago
that echoes in my bones
on the screened porch
of my mother's house

where around midnight,
wrapped in a blanket,
suitcase packed again,
I listen to the trains
pulling out of New Orleans,
heading north,
heading south.

Cold Front

> *Undertaker, please drive slow...*
> *Lord, I hate to see her go.*
> *Will the circle be unbroken...*

Flannel shadows huddle in the room,
patio plants draped with white bedsheets.
Hard freeze: her first night in the tomb.

My mother snipped the lilac blooms
then placed the vase to face the street,
her house awash in lavender perfume.

You never think it will come so soon.
You never think, but plan to meet
her at Mandina's some afternoon.

Today the obit in the *Times-Picayune*.
I bore the coffin on unsteady feet.
Flannel shadows huddle in the room

faucets drip, the wind shrieks out of tune,
windows rattle and floorboards creak.
Hard freeze: her first night in the tomb.

Mourning doves ask *who who whom?*
as morning light begins its steady seep.
Lavender shadows huddle in the room.
Cold front: her first night in the tomb.

Reading Poetry at the Maple Leaf Bar From a Book I haven't Written Yet

You know the kind of dream it was:
the ten-minutes-to-catch-a-plane-
but-I-haven't-started-packing one.

A jazz combo stands behind me,
my favorite players, and the audience
is crowded with tipsy friends, clapping,
but I forgot to bring my poems to read

and—this being a dream—I fly
to my dead mother's house
(sold years ago) to pick up a copy
of my first book, but back at the bar
when I flip open the tattered cover
I don't recognize any titles because

these are the poems I haven't written yet
growing inside me as I was once
inside her, and forgetting about
the musicians and the audience
I can't stop turning the pages in wonder,
marveling at the yet unborn words

and thinking ah yes, this one and that one!
that is the poem I've always meant to write

so I begin the reading with this.

II.

When The Saints

*I put a spell on you
because you're mine ...*

- Nina Simone, "I Put a Spell on You"

Over the Oysters

for Lee Grue

Bobby Blue Bland wipes
beads of sweat from his brow
with a big blue handkerchief
then drapes it over the mike
while back in a far corner
we have burst out crying—
birth death marriage divorce
failure success money sex—
waiters tilting to us tray
after tray of half shells
and pitcher after pitcher
of Dixie beer because here

in New Orleans feelings
are cheap and raw and opened
and we eat them by the dozen,
weeping like the Walrus
and the Carpenter over life
because we are living it,
weeping over the oysters
as one by one we swallow them,
the sea finally paying attention,
its own tears arranged in a circle,
each broken as a secret locket
and smiling slowly, we drown

as Bobby Blue Bland mops
his face, stares straight
into the spotlight
and belts out one more song.

Nasty Water

for Joanna Côte

Joanna complains that Jules
tossed out the slimy water
with the dead roses in it
she was saving to paint
a formal portrait of death,
une nature morte.

She can dry more white roses
but where is she going to get
another vase of that
nasty water?

Joanna,
let's haunt the cemetery
a week after Easter
to scoop up green scum
from the lilies rotting
in their marble urns.
Better yet, we could hide
behind the tombs waiting
for a fresh burial, tie
a string to a mason jar
then drop it down
the well into that murky
crawfish contagion
of our ancestors' bones.

Let's fill a go-cup
with the gelatinous holy
water from St. Rose
de Lima on Bayou Road.
Or next time it rains,
drain ditch gumbo
from the neutral ground
on St. Claude Avenue.

Or skim that brackish
wading pool in City Park
over by the flying horses,
the one with those bronze
angels peeing on each other,
where I pranced and splashed
feverish in my underpants
every summer while fat Nana
fanned herself with the *Dixie Roto*
under the shade of live oaks.

We can't miss the monkey pond
at the Audubon Park Zoo
putrid with peanut shells,
doodlebugs, and baboon bottoms,
or the porticoed seal pool
where dead mackerel are tossed
at high noon in the middle
of August to seal pups
too plump to roll over.

Or the ducks, we can always
go feed the ducks near
the solemn stone lions
at the City Park lagoon
and siphon off some
black tadpole broth
where swans preen
in mean perfection
and stale bread crusts
bob, bloat, and sink
among mosquito hawks.

Nasty water? You say
you want nasty water?

New Orleans is a shimmering
mirage floating on nasty water,
irrigated by nasty water,
nasty water seeping out
of every pore, steeping
in crab grass on the levee
like a bitter green tea
then trickling in rivulets
down to that Queen of Nasty
Water, the Mississippi,
Gaia of primordial funk,
mother of us all. We drink
her, brew her, cook her up
into okra gumbo, into
a lifelong Scorpionic
soup of afterbirths
and Extreme Unctions,
secretions and
family secrets:

nasty water,
nasty water,
"proud to call it home."

Crabs in the Hamper

It's my large God-like metal pincers
versus their small briny blue claws
locked onto each others' in a clacking
cluster inside the Styrofoam cooler.

The living cling to each other on top
of the dead fallen to the bottom, rising
to battle this shopper's poking tongs.
They will not budge, snarled into a ball

like bomb survivors in an air-raid shelter,
school kids during a shooting lockdown.
What new hell is this? crabs must wonder.
Soon they'll be back among the waves

feasting on a turkey neck in the trap, soon
they'll scuttle along the shore in moonlight.
But should one try to escape the cooler
the ever wary claws of the others pull it

back down. Come trap, come hamper,
or the pincers of an all too arbitrary fate,
they won't release each other: *don't leave us,*
they beseech, until the cauldron has boiled

roiling with laurel leaves, and in that final second
they let go, sliding into broth seasoned like the sea.

Acts of God

Outside, rowboats paddled up Canal Street
while I was delivered howling by lantern
in a hospital called Hôtel Dieu during
a hurricane that knocked out New Orleans.
I have a feel for rattling window panes,
for rivers racing through sky, for heaven

flung endlessly down. This year August ends
with God banging on the door like the police.
Venetian blinds clatter against glass,
gusts ripple through calendar pages back
to the day of my birth, the steel wok hung
by a hook from the rafter chimes an Angelus

against the skillet, curtains billow as I
follow from bed to bed, room to room, city
to city, continent to continent, capturing
the wind like a spinnaker, covering weather
maps with cyclonic swirls and arrows, over-
flowing boundaries, sexes, and time zones.

My kitchen globe brightens as the sky blackens
and rising with the steam of a boiling kettle
I approach my glory, the air finally matching
my emergency, reaching for the same velocity,
announcing ourselves with a loosened shutter
back and forth against the side of the house.

(September, 2005)

Superdome Lullaby

The writer lost his verbs
and the painter lost her hues,
the drag queen lost her wigs
and the gardener lost his beds.

The dentist lost his patients,
his patients lost their teeth,
the butcher lost their business
because they couldn't chew.

The rain lost its gutters
and the gutters lost their roof,
the roof lost its chimney
and the chimney lost its sky.

The auntie lost her life
on the rockabilly roof.
Her children lost their boat
as the baby floated by.

The sugar lost its spoon
and the rice lost its beans.
The lightning lost its fork
and the surgeon lost his knife.

New Orleans lost its people
and I lost my longneck joy.
Listen, child, while I sing about
where your daddy used to live.

(September, 2005)

A Blind Lady Singing

in front of Walgreens,
face screwed up into
a pale wrinkled sun
in the rain on Royal.
"Those were the days,

my friends"—O the actors,
the theaters, the poets,
the readings, the painters,
the galleries—"we thought
they'd never end."

The French Quarter is shut down,
Canal Street an ashen ghost town.
Hail the conquering CEOs
from Haliburton and FEMA
triumphant in a tourist buggy.

"We'd fight and never lose."
I hurry past the blind lady
singing on Royal Street
pouring out her heart
filled with
rain.

(October, 2005)

From Below, From Above

While we're raising the roof
they're busy eating beneath
the floor we're standing on:
underground mountain of pale
larvae, a souk of devilish
appetite chewing, chewing,
undoing the beams of dawn.

In morning light we mount
the day so purposefully,
our work already undone
by those who lurk in shadows
inside the hives of holocausts
we tread upon, until one fine day

the banister is marshmallow,
joists turned to peanut brittle.
Termites flutter from slits in
kitchen walls while above,
the long-buried chrysalis
of a death wish sprouts wings.

Two black birds attack the towers:
destruction swarms from simple things,
floors, windows, suitcases, flights home.
Underneath they're chewing, chewing
humble mouthfuls in hollow places
while above ground we're framing

buildings that almost touch the sky.

(September, 2001)

KING MIDAS BLUES

We have prayed for
the power. Now it's ours.
Everything we touch
turns to smudge.

From the Alaskan coast
to the Gulf of Mexico,
everywhere we go
turns to sludge.

From the exhaust-pipe air
to the flaming oil wells
on our Iraqi victory cake,
every horizon blurs to smog.

BP gold, Texaco gold,
dolphins and pelicans,
the turtles in the bayou
are slick with black gold.

Golden-haired, our most
loved daughter lies dying
of cancer at twenty-six
with petrochemical cells.

We have killed for
the power. Now it's ours.
Everything we own
turns to poison.

(April, 2010)

Pelicans Feeding

for my teachers

On land they are as ridiculous
as a poet defending his profession
to the IRS, or a busted umbrella
ambulant on two plastic spatulas.

In midair their pterodactyl wingspan
looms sacramental, necks as delicately
curved in flight as an African carving.
They skim above breakers, cresting

and falling with the sea's cadence
then rising, they plunge in nonchalant
circles, flipping into a perpendicular
dive. With honed eye intent they pluck

the living poem from just beneath
the same surface you and I were scanning
in bored disquiet, then nip and gargle
the thrashing word, bobbing up and down.

And from my teachers I've learned as much
as by watching the pelicans feed at dusk.

Spell for this First Kiss

Dust swept from under the beds
of the nine seas I have crossed.
Clover plucked from the crevices
of my tomb in St. Louis Cemetery.

Smiles of those I've loved cut out,
collaged into a diamond question mark.
A song replayed thirty-three times:
Ne me quitte pas, ne me quitte pas.

A hot oyster po'boy shared on
the gallery, a black cat rubbing
its back against the rusty screen.
Fragrance of wet rattan, fallen

figs, the first August rains
under the live oaks in City Park.
A lavender rose on the dashboard
of a car waiting for a draw-

bridge to open, to let sail past
this first kiss: streamlined
as ships that navigate the world
bringing you to places

you have no business being—
until you drink this potion,
wake, look into my eyes—
and the hieroglyphs make sense.

French Quarter Bar Fugue
Corner St. Louis and Chartres Then Down to Decatur

1
Maspero's Exchange

Great grandpère
Glaudot
sold cigars
at Maspero's.
At dusk his darkie
cook would go
barefoot down
the Esplanade
to Rampart past
the slave exchange.

He married Mémère off
to Tennessee society
but kept the younger sister home
for bedpan work and normal school
and to lug the sideboard crystal set
from eight to four room vacancies.

Dark, dark is the stain
left at Maspero's Exchange.
The walls are white and
pastel champagne bubbles
fizzle from the tipping tumbler
tattooed on the barroom
window panes

so black the stain.

Inside a silky bouffant Negro
tilts a tray of drinks to tables.
Above his smoothly vermouth movements
attic woodwork worms with vermin,

generations cotton-fed and fat
nest inside the skull of Maspero
and the enamel pitcher of père Glaudot,
these glints of paleness embering
around the sockets swilling darkness

while downstairs there is flickering
some antique dance upon the walls,
thick peels of whitewash flaking
with the heat of summer nights.

2

Napoleon House

Wood strum the waiter
from the door to the bar,
that aristocratic penguin
in the looped bowtie,
toothless, listless,
with the shoe-shined grace
of the emperor who never
showed up but died
on St. Helena while the Creoles schemed.

Napoleon, Napoleon,
you maudlin melancholian,
slumped against the table
in a dignified drunk,
spectacles fallen
into your beer,
wishing you were anywhere else
but here.

In winter I remember
a corner wrapped in amber

and Brahms that swirled
around the room
like brandy in a goblet
and summer-feathered light that fell
like ferns upon the patio
where glasses emptied slowly.

Time rides the heavy mahogany blades
of the lugubrious overhead fan
that drags thoughts in a drugged whir
down toward the chink of ice floating
in the foam of a brandy Alexander.
The waiter eternally polishing glass
and reading a yellowed newssheet
stands ceramically still near the clock
that always reads midnight or noon

while all around are lingering
in antique portraits on the walls
glares of exiled princes waiting
swift returns to buried thrones.

3
The Acropolis

Opium Rose
swings her milk-thick tits
in Greek juke rhythms.
Both of them are mothers
but she's been fixed.
In stretching pink cashmere
she scoops up bottles,
empties ashtrays
and slow eyes sailors
with a parched ruby smile.

Behind the bar
she smashes glass
and pours out ouzo
then kicks her way
through oyster shells.
She knows the words
but seldom sings them.

While college twiglets
jingle metal bracelets
and tap their feet
to the *Zeibékiko*
(the dance meant
only for one man)
and Aegean shadows
unfurl against lime neon
to hiss, swoop, and swallow
in their strange ballet

the checkered belt-loop dates
disappear into the men's room
where around the Greek graffiti
they find a plastic lily
jammed into the vent
of the prophylactics machine.

My Wild Lover

in memory, French Quarter bohemia

Montmartre en ce temps-là...
On était jeunes, on était fous...
  -Charles Aznavour, "La Bohème"

At that moment when drunken
lips meet, cats purr
and chocolate melts, the fullness
that is—after all—only a moment
I think of you, purple-
mouthed Dionysius crowned
with laurels in a bath-towel
toga, your impish glee
at nipples and pastel pens,
with your disheveled mop
of Biblical curls, raising
a jug of Paisano during one
of your impromptu spaghetti feasts
(you invited everyone you met)
and proclaiming something silly
but earth-shattering before
you wound the maroon muffler
around your gold corduroy coat
like the Little Prince and were off again
past the Greek sailors on Decatur Street

into another woman's arms.
Picture me now, a grandmother
alone with the Internet
and a bottle of Chardonnay,
the sepulchral green lawn
spilling toward my window,
memory choked with weeds.
I feel sorry for the wives
who tried to browbeat you into
this, the housebroken drudges

we've become. I had the best
of you—all your far-flung
friends and lovers did. Our glass
was always filled, now the hourglass
has emptied, and we lower you into
scrapbooks: I loved you more
than the men who stayed with me
and lasted well past fullness,
down to the bitter dregs.
You are the shock of sun
on a sallow cheek after
the day is done. You are
the moment we live for

and this is the rest.

Iron Lace

The delicately rococo swirls
of wrought-iron galleries
along French Quarter streets

are exactingly intricate filigrees
of patience and passion and work.
Visitors stand back three feet

careful not to crush the curlicues
while a little boy swings free
as a monkey from his balcony.

Conquistadors with horses
French with fancy carriages
Americans with automobiles

have shoved and plowed against
these finest of iron string quartets.
Still they are here, teasingly fragile,

a wise disguise of three centuries
we wear like a glove, a wisp of smoke.
But iron to the bone. Crowds come

and they go while we preside over
the centennials of live oak trees.
Lean on us.
    Iron lace does not break.

Nietzsche in Disneyland

Americans become their cartoons:
pastel gaggles of pudgy ducks
with pert baseball-cap bills
waddle at a calliope gait

through the French Quarter.
The world is their theme park,
a padded polka-dot Garden
of Eden three off-ramps

beyond good and evil.
Like water, history rolls
off them into dank drains.
Wry Creole ghosts peer

down from rusted balconies
like Nietzsche in Disneyland
as adult-sized toddlers
with iPhone eyes float by

on a river of cheap beer.

HITTING THE CARNIVAL WALL

Our bus driver is a maniac
who tests positive for marijuana.
Speed jammed at ninety an hour,
crammed in on top of each other,
all we can do is get drunk.
We each become somebody else
to everyone's great relief.

Suddenly we slam into a brick
wall of cops and garbage trucks.
Goggle-eyed rag dolls, we collapse
in a heap on some stranger's bed.
Tattered costumes peel off
as we stomp through a swamp
of smashed beer cans. The driver
is a sack of empty tequila bottles
dragged off by a long white apron.

Wednesday, priests replace police.
Brushing off cobwebs of confetti,
we are frog-marched one
by one through a turnstile
onto a desert of ash
that takes forty days to cross
on foot to the next town,
where azaleas blossom along broad
magenta esplanades, the driver

is revived and all is forgiven.

The Princess of Banana Leaves and Rain

At any moment
strolling through New Orleans
a gray rat snake may drop on you
from a gnarled live oak overhead,
whose branches stretch out
from a haze of Spanish moss
like an old man rising
from a murky bath
of dreams.

Here, where white
cemeteries of toadstools
glisten on lawns after summer showers,
sex and death conspire, are married
together by the lascivious priests
of dark water and dense heat
in week-long ceremonies
that inspire vast
throngs

and headlines:
LOVE NEST OF THE AX MURDERESS!
BEHEADED CORPSE OF STAR GODDESS!
A dizzy conspiracy theory of presidential
assassins begins to unravel
while a skeleton tangos
with a rose clenched
between its teeth
at Carnival.

The hermit nun,
given as her life's work
the contemplation of a human skull,
plays riverboat calliope inside walls
of the deserted convent garden

while her brothers, the belly-
dancing, bourbon belting
monks make the sign
of the cross

with wrought-iron
phalluses under the grille window
of the princess of banana leaves and rain.
The Mississippi twists through the locks
of Medusa, and under the river's skin
the fat coils of enormous
water moccasins, covered
with eons of silt,
writhe slowly,
slowly

in a jazz funeral
of perpetual decay.

Lament on the Assassination Six Days Later
with lyrics by New Orleans blues musician Babe Stovall

Time Lord time Lord

Already shop windows glossed thick with photographs,
Martin Luther King Jr. tumblers, recordings, tee-shirts,
handkerchiefs and memorial ashtrays shaped like America
with embossed ceramic banners spouting "I Have a Dream,"
glazed green, with a few cigarettes ground out
in uncontainable fistfuls of scattering ashes.

time is a winding up

Commemoration mumbles and is gone.
Streets are hosed by vinyl yellow trolls, lined
with buckets of lime, and handcuffed by rows
of the pearl-helmeted insect eyes of the squad.
Downtown faces black with mourning camel walk
the drugstore parking lot, combing the crowd
for smokes while frantic men in serge pajamas
stack bones in the basement intoning the monotone
of oversight and fumbling with their futures.
Schoolchildren are sent hollering home for a holiday
of parental muteness behind double-latched doors
while hymns from the Baptist church next door
rise in great fluttering robes to cover the sky.

time Lord time Lord time is a winding up

Confederate hero Jefferson Davis hunches
his brackish bronze shoulders to the spring,
wears a joke mourning band around his neck,
tailcoat smudged with tracks of tiny footprints.

Lord there destruction in this land

A tune tinkles on slow wheels down the street

as Harmony sticks to fingers, drips from under sun hats.
Sympathy stands knock-kneed as a mannequin
posed to announce a hurried sale
and oblations of discounted roses
clog the doorway of Kresge's.

and God gonna move his hand

On the Canal Street bus I watch
apocalyptic billboard stallions gallop
through the wrinkles in the tinted
safety glass of public transit.
Next to me, textbooks in lap,
a black high school student scans
the assassination in the pages
of a magazine that now seem
nothing more than something else
that's white.

when time goes winding up

(April 10, 1968)

MR. BOUDREAUX'S CIVIL WAR

Under a leaky washtub sky
galvanized to the horizon,
I ride shotgun in a pickup
with Mr. Boudreaux, "half-ass
coon-ass,"

      specialist
in hate. He even knows
that Hungarians in Baltimore
were called "hunkies
the coons mispronounced
as honkies."

      Half Grosse Tête
and half Polish, he looks like
the Pope in baggy seersucker
shorts and a tee-shirt
that says something.

      So it goes
between Lafayette and New Orleans,
hearing about his twenty guns
and his new civil war:
"the niggers vs. us, winner
take all."

He's going to pick off
a few before he dies. His only son
stuck a pistol into his dumb drunk
mouth and blew his brains out.
He weeps, windshield wipers
smearing blood

      and Budweiser
across the darkening sky

as we pass through
gnarled cypress swamps.
In his florid face
I make out

        blotchy maps
of Bosnia and Rwanda,
the partition of India,
six million neighbors
dead in railway cars.
This enemy is

        so close
we share a Bud, a place,
a language and a Saint Day:
he's the father-in-law
of the niece of my mother's
friend,

        a stranger I've hired
to haul my great-grandparents'
furniture, a truckload of chipped
prie-dieus, rickety armoires,
and rocking chairs with busted
cane seats

        where generations
were nursed: madonnas
with haloes of termites.
Bumping along with Mr. Boudreaux
I don't recognize the road ahead,
only childhood

        feet up
in the rearview mirror.

I've been playing hooky
and he's carrying me
back into history,
here

     where the grainy
black-and-white light
needs no foreign subtitles,
where the air is bruised,
heavy with accumulated
grievance

        and I—
for lack of a better word,
a better world—
belong.

Solomon's Sword, or the Café au Lait Blues

Cinnamon skin and green eyes:

    Don't know who the mama is
    and not sure of the daddy.
    But he's ours, he's ours
    this beautiful brown baby.

He makes Mardi Gras black

    my French ancestors
    would raise their brows
    at the very idea
    of a Zulu Ball

and jazz white

    your African ancestors
    would split a rib
    to see this pink man
    second-line.

Can't say who the mama is
and not sure of the daddy:

    You write sniffing Whitman
    while I write sipping Langston.
    And what Chopin does to you
    James Booker does for me.

Cinnamon skin and green eyes:

    Sheath the sword
    that would slice this child
    in two. Ours, New Orleans,
    let's call him ours,
    this beautiful brown baby.

What Remains

in New Orleans is a bloodhound
scent, secretive as boyhood,
of alleys and damp clay,
a shadow lengthening into

a procession of generations
disappearing under the gnarled
oak fingers of Esplanade Avenue.
And the wound of history

reopened as a souvenir shop,
a denial long as the levee,
bottomless as the swamp we
climbed up from—brick

by slippery brick—along
the bent backs of slaves.
And the last marble petal
of a disheveled family rose

waiting in the whitewashed
sunlight for my name and dates.

Impossible Cases

Anonymous as the skull-white altar.
As the separate votive tongues
pulsing a fugue in unison
in the darkness.
                As hands clasped
together next to mine. As sin—
or whatever they call this whiff
of mortality, like meat
starting to go bad.
                Anonymous
as prayers I stumble through, prompted
by the lady next to me who doesn't know
why I'm here, and I—no better about her—
but we're related
                because death,
anonymous as dirt, gets all over
everything. And because I am I
and another unnamed animal dying
I come to you,
                St. Jude,
stop to search for a crack
in the rock where your anchor
catches, but am not entirely taken in,
see the seams
                of this holy show: wheezing,
a sexton stacks crates of dollar candles,
a mother shushes her shrill child,
hoisting him to touch the plaster hem
then hurrying out.
                Which he'll forget—
if he's lucky—or will it all come back
in fifty years in a grim hotel room
God-knows-where, the bearded saint
afloat a sea of candles?
                Already,

anonymously, he has joined us
kneeling. His quarters rock
in the offering box
                    as the anchor drops.

Busted Flat in Baton Rouge

Driving through darkening bayous
I listen to Janis Joplin croak and cackle,
banjos strumming among cypress knees.
A cone-headed African goddess
windswept carmine across the sky
conjures with elegant fingers,
swirling marionette strings
to raise the dead from the swamp.

Bones leap up like a Baptist
resurrection, jangling joints
that don't stay dead for long
until land conspires with sky,
light with clouds, descending:
spirit returns to place and date
surely as a Pharaoh's craggy face
emerges from a pudding of baby fat.

Stooped shadows amped-up and humming
surround me, the tomb where I've buried
love after careless love cracking open,
hips swaying, knees and elbows bending.
Ghost mouths twenty and sweet
as moon pies sing inside me
like a dead girl tossing
her hair into car wind
down Interstate 10.

In Lieu of Flowers

After I die
no more erections,
no more wild parties
for anyone, okay?
No more bagels
on Sunday morning,
no more sprawling
in afternoon sunlight.
I want you to suffer.
My body will be rotting
in a brick box on Esplanade
so from then on, oatmeal
for you, homespun and
cold showers. No more
smoking, drinking, staying
up late. The good old days
officially will be over.
Do your taxes on New Year's Eve.
Darn your socks on Mardi Gras.

You'll finally have a great excuse
to mope, so go ahead, be morose.
Order bottled water. Become a vegan.
You could never keep up
with my leaps of joy
so stay on the ground floor
and watch the planes take off
for luscious destinations.

I'll be in the cockpit,
gulping champagne and
French-kissing the copilot
but you—
         wipe that smile
off your face.

After I die
I'll have my eye
 on you.

Visit to the Memory Unit

"Summers in Waveland, there were two houses,
one for the boys, another for the girls...."
Black orderlies in starched white wheel
meal carts inside the reflecting glass.
In the courtyard of Château de Notre Dame,
silver perm cocked coquettishly, she chants,
"In summer, in Waveland, always two houses,

one for boys...." I go over with her
addresses we lived at, dishes cooked,
dates of deaths. "And one for girls.
In summer. In Waveland. When it rained..."
she explains, clutching a purse that contains
room key, meal ticket, snapshot of plantation
grandeur bleached by thumbprints.

We maneuver the labyrinthine paths along
sculptured shrubs, she leaning on my arm.
Later I run drunk the exile-crowded streets
where my aunt once led me by the hand.
I walk to remember as she walks to forget
and we meet—almost as if by chance—
here in circles at the end of time.

WAVELAND

after Neruda

Whitecaps, hurricane weather on the Gulf
with wave after wave heaving to shatter
its whiteness, the ocean's bottomless cup
brimming over, the motioning sky slashed
by long slow swoops of sacerdotal birds.
Then the yellow appears,
September changes color growing
a beard of coastal autumn
and I—my name's the same,
I haven't changed,
I'm in love, I'm in doubt,
I'm in debt,
I have the enormous Gulf,
its workers piling wave on wave,
and such a stormy nature
I visit nations not born yet:
I come and I go from the sea
and its countries where I know
the spiny-finned Indian languages
and the teeth of Iberian fish,
the shiver of Himalayan altitudes,
Thai coral blood and the solemn
Chinese night of the whale—
because I journeyed from land to land,
through estuaries, the remotest regions,
but I always came back. I found no peace.
What could I say without my roots?

What could I say without touching the earth?
To whom should I speak but the rain?
Wherever I was, I was never really there,
I never traveled anywhere but the way here
and from the grand cathedrals I treasured
no postcards or souvenirs: with open hands
I've tried to found my stone,

reasonably, unreasonably, with extravagance,
with fury and balance: at every turn
I trespassed on the lion's lair
and the bee's tumultuous tower.
So when I saw what I once called my own,
when I touched ground, my stone and foam,
beings that recognize my steps, my voice,
vines that kissed my lips, I whispered
"I'm home"
                 and standing stripped in daylight
let my hands slip down into the water
and when everything was as clear
under the earth, I was quiet.

Acknowledgments

I would like to acknowledge with gratitude the source of the book's cover image, a photograph by Sandra Russell Clark from the "Greenwood" section of her book *Elysium: A Gathering of Souls* (Louisiana State University Press). I also thank Kathleen Grieshaber for her patient assistance with the photograph's colorization and the cover design. Once again I am grateful to James D. Wilson, editor at the University of Louisiana at Lafayette Press, for his careful work in producing this collection.

The following poems have appeared in these previous collections: *Why I Live in the Forest* (Wesleyan University Press, 1974): "Return to the House of Scorpio," "Mardi Gras Grandmothers," "The Shoebox," "Presenting Eustacia Beauchaud: Rosary 3," "Tyger! Tyger!," "French Quarter Bar Fugue"; *What Moves Is Not the Wind* (Wesleyan University Press, 1980): "Judgment," "Sum"; *Drunk on Salt* (Willow Springs Editions, 2014): "The Invention of Hands on Columbus Street," "Dead Man's Float," "Acts of God," "From Below, from Above," "My Wild Lover," "The Princess of Banana Leaves and Rain," "Impossible Cases," "In Lieu of Flowers."

"Nasty Water" originally appeared as a broadside published by L-Pantheon Press.

In various versions, these poems were first published in the following anthologies and magazines:

Adam among the Television Trees: An Anthology of Verse by Contemporary Christian Poets (ed. Virginia R. Mollenkott, Word Books): "Locked in a Home for *les Enfants Dérangés par Dieu*"
Big Bridge (Crescent City Issue): "From Below, from Above"
Callaloo: A Journal of African Diaspora Arts and Letters: "Acts of God," "A Blind Lady Singing"
Chance of a Ghost: An Anthology of Contemporary Ghost Poems (eds. Gloria Vando and Philip Miller, Helicon Nine Editions): "In Lieu of Flowers"
Chatahoochee Review: "Time Explains, Among Other Things"
Double Dealer Redux: "The American Century"
From a Bend in the River: 100 New Orleans Poets (ed. Kalamu ya

Salaam, Runagate Press): "Nasty Water"
Hogtown Creek Review: "Home Blues"
Improbable Worlds: An Anthology of Texas and Louisiana Poets (ed. Martha Serpas, Mutabilis Press): "Impossible Cases"
The Jazz Poetry Anthology (eds. Yusef Komunyakaa and Sacha Feinstein, Indiana University Press): "Presenting Eustacia Beauchaud: Rosary 3"
Maple Leaf Rag III: An Anthology of Poetic Writings from the Maple Leaf Reading Series (ed. John Travis, Portals Press): "Acts of God"
Maple Leaf Rag IV: "In the Rotunda"
Maple Leaf Rag V: "Home Blues," "Reading Poetry at the Maple Leaf Bar from a Book I Haven't Written Yet"
Meena: A Bilingual Journal of Arts and Letters: "King Midas Blues"
Mesachabe: A Journal of Surregionalism: "Dream Castle (1964)"
Michigan Quarterly Review: "Japanese Plums"
My New Orleans: Ballads to the Big Easy by Her Sons, Daughters, and Lovers (ed. Rosemary James, Simon & Schuster): "Nasty Water"
My Shameless St. Augustine Scrapbook (ed. Ruth Moon Kempler, Kings Estate Press): "Pelicans Feeding"
New American Review 13 (ed. Theodore Solotaroff, Simon & Schuster): "Sum"
New Laurel Review: "Nasty Water," "My Wild Lover"
New Orleans Review: "Acts of God," "Impossible Cases," "Waveland" (sections 12 and 13 of my version of Pablo Neruda's "Fin de fiesta")
Quarry West: "The Invention of Hands on Columbus Street"
Quimera: Revista de Literatura (Barcelona): "Mardi Gras Grandmothers," "The Invention of Hands on Columbus Street" (with translation into Spanish by José Luis Regojo)
The Southern Poetry Anthology, Volume IV: Louisiana (eds. Paul Ruffin and William Wright, Texas Review Press): "Over the Oysters," "Acts of God," "King Midas Blues"
Stringtown: "Hunt & Peck"
Upward Bound Newspaper (Eckerd College, Summer 1968): "Lament on the Assassination Six Days Later"
Xavier Review: "Shotgun Nocturne for Those Who Left"
YAWP: Journal of Poetry: "Spell for This First Kiss"

JAMES NOLAN, a fifth-generation New Orleans native, is a widely published fiction writer, poet, essayist, and translator. His eleventh book, *Flight Risk: Memoirs of a New Orleans Bad Boy*, won the 2018 Next-Generation Indie Book Award for Best Memoir. His fiction includes *You Don't Know Me: New and Selected Stories* (winner of the 2015 Independent Publishers Gold Medal in Southern Fiction), the novel *Higher Ground* (awarded a Faulkner/Wisdom Gold Medal), and *Perpetual Care: Stories*. He has been the recipient of an N.E.A. grant and two Fulbright fellowships, and has taught at universities in San Francisco, Florida, Barcelona, Madrid, and Beijing, as well as in New Orleans.

www.ingramcontent.com/pod-product-compliance
Lightning Source LLC
Chambersburg PA
CBHW020127130526
44591CB00032B/561